Wood

To those who helped birth this book: Jane Yolen for her brilliant guidance, Christina Pulles for sharing my vision, Natascha Morris for believing in me, the Penguins and Scribblers for insights and camaraderie, and my family for all else.—T.R.

The author would like to thank Sharon Bertsch McGrayne for permission to use a quote from Wu Chien Shiung's family.

union
square
kids

**NEW YORK**

UNION SQUARE KIDS and the distinctive Union Square Kids logo are trademarks of Union Square & Co., LLC.

Union Square & Co., LLC, is a subsidiary of Sterling Publishing Co., Inc.

ISBN 978-1-4549-3220-8

Library of Congress Cataloging-in-Publication Data
Names: Robeson, Teresa, 1964- author. | Huang, Rebecca, illustrator.
Title: Queen of physics : how Wu Chien Shiung helped unlock the secrets of the atom / Teresa Robeson ; illustrated by Rebecca Huang.
Description: New York, NY : Sterling Children's Books, [2019] | Audience:5 & up | Audience: K to 3.
Identifiers: LCCN 2019010214| ISBN 9781454932208 (hardcover) | ISBN 1454932201 (hardcover)
Subjects: LCSH: Wu, C. S. (Chien-shiung), 1912-1997--Juvenile literature.| Nuclear physicists--United States--Biography--Juvenile literature. | Women physicists--Biography--Juvenile literature. | Chinese Americans--Biography--Juvenile literature.
Classification: LCC QC16.W785 R63 2019 | DDC 530.092 [B] --dc23

For information about custom editions, special sales, and premium purchases, please contact specialsales@unionsquareandco.com.

Printed in China

Lot #:
8  10  9  7

06/23

unionsquareandco.com

Design by Julie Robine

# Queen of Physics

## How WU CHIEN SHIUNG
## Helped Unlock the Secrets of the Atom

written by
Teresa Robeson

illustrated by Rebecca Huang

union
square
kids

NEW YORK

In China, in the small town of Liuhe,
the Wu family celebrated the birth of a child.

The child was a girl.

A girl!

What would
become of her?

In those days,

girls were not sent to school,
not considered as smart as boys,
and certainly not encouraged to be scientists.

But Mama and Baba Wu did not feel that way.
They believed girls should go to school
and could become anything they wanted to be.

They knew their daughter would be smart and brave, that she would make a difference in the world.

Baba named her Chien Shiung, which means "courageous hero."

Even before Wu Chien Shiung
arrived in the world,
Baba had quit his job as an engineer
and opened a school just for girls.

Mama wore out her shoes trudging to every house in Liuhe
to urge families to educate their daughters.

So when Chien Shiung was ready, a school was waiting for her.

Baba was the principal and Mama the teacher,
teaching little girls to read
and write
and count.

Baba and Mama were courageous, too, as they showed their daughter the way.

Soon enough, Chien Shiung had
learned everything she could from
her parents' school.
She knew how to count—
and to add, subtract, multiply, divide.
She knew how to read and write—
hundreds of Chinese words
with their strong dots, angled lines,
and wispy tails.

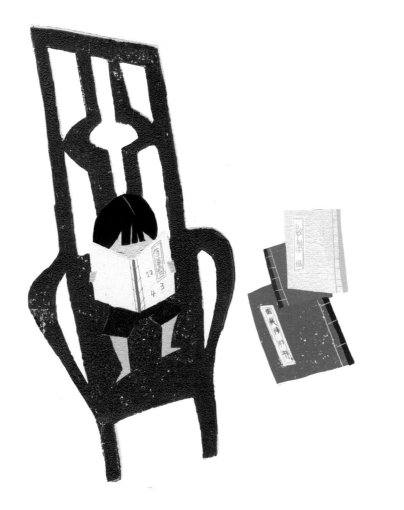

Chien Shiung was ready for more!

But in the 1920s, the next
closest girls' school
was in the city of Suzhou,
fifty long miles of bumpy,
dusty country roads away.
She would have to live there,
far from her family,
and could only go home for
winter and summer vacations.

Mama wept.
Baba worried.
But they knew their
daughter had to brave
the world to grow.

Chien Shiung knew it, too.
So off she went.

The school offered two programs:
teacher training and academic.
Chien Shiung picked the free teacher training program,
but she peeked into the academic program textbooks
and saw that they covered so much more.

Science wasn't just science;

it was biology,

and chemistry,

and physics,

all connected by the lovely language of mathematics.

And, oh, physics!
Physics, the study of the very matter
and energy around her,
the study of things that could be seen or felt
   —heat, sound, light, electricity, and motion—
and of things too minuscule to be seen or felt
   —atoms and even tinier parts of atoms.
Physics captured her heart.

$F=ma$

$$\frac{dV}{dt} = \sum_i F_i = 0$$

During the day, Chien Shiung attended her own classes.
At night, she studied the academic textbooks she borrowed from friends.
She called it "self-learning."
It was a habit she would keep up for the rest of her life.

Her classmates noticed that Chien Shiung worked extra hard and was not afraid of challenges. They asked her to be their leader in their "underground" group to fight against the government. Citizens were not allowed to say what they wanted. If they supported the wrong political party, or said the wrong thing, or happened to be at the wrong place at the wrong time, they could be punished—perhaps even killed—by the government, by the warlords, by rich and powerful foreigners who lived there.

The students wanted someone brave to lead them.
They asked Chien Shiung.

What would she do? What *could* she do?

Baba had named her "courageous hero."
She would live up to her name.

With her days full of classes, homework,
secret studying on her own,
and leading student protests and strikes,
Chien Shiung had little time to miss her family.

The years flew by.

Now seventeen years old, she graduated with top grades.
It would have been easy to go home,
but she took the harder path and traveled to Nanjing—
three times farther from home than she had *ever* gone before—
to attend the National Central University
where she immersed herself in her favorite subject, physics.

保衛中華

堅持抗日

Once again her hard work and determination
made her a leader among the students.
Wu Chien Shiung led the march to
General Chiang Kai Shek's headquarters,
where she and her classmates
urged his government to resist Japanese
invaders just before the start of World War II.

Like a seed that must fly far to flourish,
Chien Shiung set forth once more in 1936,
this time to Berkeley, California, thousands
of miles across the ocean.
She was going to continue studying the
physics of atoms.

Scientists understood atoms,
but not completely.
If people knew how atoms
split, they could use them
in new inventions and
technologies, maybe even help
doctors treat sick people.

She focused on *beta decay*,
where a nucleon inside an atom
broke into an opposite nucleon,
an electron or positron,
and a neutrino.
It was like opening one present
and getting three different gifts inside.

After California, Chien Shiung went to Columbia University in New York, where she continued to explore beta decay.

She was careful.

She was precise.

She conducted experiment after experiment until she had a deeper understanding of beta decay than just about anyone else.
Her reputation grew, and physicists who couldn't solve their own problems came to her for help.

Scientist Enrico Fermi said that electrons should have had faster speeds when they burst out of the neutron during beta decay.
He couldn't prove it.
Nobody could.

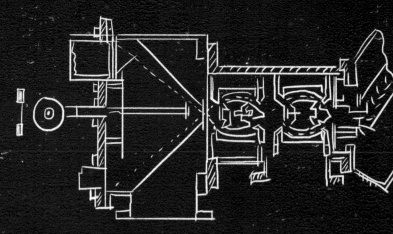

But Chien Shiung could!

Because she understood beta decay so well,
she knew what to look for.
Because she was such a careful researcher,
she was able to run a difficult experiment
that proved Fermi right.

Many people thought that Chien Shiung should have won the Nobel Prize for this work, but she did not receive it.

When two physicists, Yang Chen Ning and Lee Tsung Dao, questioned something many scientists believed—that nature did not distinguish between right and left, a concept of symmetry called *parity*—they asked Chien Shiung to investigate.

Because she had worked on parity in beta decay, she knew just what to do. To focus on the project, she even cancelled a trip to China, a rare chance to see her parents for the first time since she had left home for the United States.

Her hard work paid off:
her results proved them right!

For this, Yang and Lee,
but *not* Chien Shiung,
won a Nobel Prize.

Another two physicists, Richard Feynman and Murray Gell-Mann,
asked her to check their *hypothesis* about a special expression of beta decay.
In her usual thorough way, Chien Shiung ran experiments
and confirmed their idea.

Many scientists praised her for this important finding.
Yet, for the third time, she did not get the Nobel Prize.

Sometimes Chien Shiung did not get the jobs she wanted either—
because she was a woman,
because she was Asian.

Was she sad? Yes.
Was she disappointed? Often.
Was she discouraged? Occasionally.

But she did not let those feelings stop
her from doing what she loved, because
Baba always said,
"Ignore the obstacles.
Just put your head down and
keep walking forward."

There was only one obstacle she could not overcome.

Because of World War II,
the political unrest in China afterward,
and her focus on her work,
Chien Shiung was not able to return to
see her parents before they died.

"My heart was breaking," she wrote to a friend when she could not attend Baba's funeral.

Still, in her new home in the United States,
Chien Shiung continued on her courageous path.
She fought prejudice against women and Asians
and became such an exceptional physicist that
the *Smithsonian* magazine called her "The First Lady of Physics Research"
and *Newsweek* declared her the "Queen of Physics."

And that is how a small girl from a faraway village in China

went to school,

proved herself as smart as any boy,

learned to be a scientist,

and even became a queen!

The First Lady
of Physics Research

# Wu Chien Shiung's Story

Born on May 31, 1912, in the small town of Liuhe near Shanghai, China, Wu Chien Shiung (*Wu* was her last name and *Chien Shiung*, her given name) grew up in a loving family with her parents and two brothers. Unlike many parents at that time, her mother and father believed that girls were equal to boys and should have an education just like boys. They encouraged her to persevere despite the prejudice against women. This perseverance also helped her when she faced the same bias against minorities in the U.S. They believed, and taught her to believe, that she could succeed at anything she wanted. As an adult, she encouraged other girls to become scientists, too.

Wu Chien Shiung, or Madame Wu, as her students called her, accomplished amazing things. Besides performing experiments that proved beta decay and disproved the Law of Parity, she was also:

- the first woman to be hired as an instructor by Princeton University
- the first woman to receive an honorary doctorate from Princeton University
- the first woman to be elected president of The American Physical Society, in 1975
- the first scientist to have an asteroid named after her while she was still alive
- the first person to receive the Wolf Prize in Physics, in 1978

Not only was she the first woman to do these things, she was the first *Chinese* woman to achieve these honors. It is no wonder *Newsweek* magazine called her the queen of physics (May 20, 1963; issue 61, 20).

Wu died on February 16, 1997, in New York City.

# Glossary

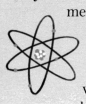

**Physics**, from the Greek word *physika*, which means "natural things," is the study of matter and energy. What exactly is matter? Why does matter act the way it does? How is energy created? Can we control energy? How are matter and energy related, and how do they work together? These are some of the many questions that physicists try to answer.

**atom**: Everything around you—including you, your house, Earth, the sun—is made of atoms. They are the smallest bits of elements, such as hydrogen and carbon, that still hold the characteristics of an element. We borrowed the word *atomos*, which means "indivisible," from the Greek language. People used to think that an atom was the tiniest bit of matter you could get if you kept cutting something into smaller and smaller pieces. But now we know that is not true. As tiny as an atom is, it is made up of even tinier parts: neutrons, protons, and electrons.

**beta decay**: Also written as "β decay" by scientists, beta decay is basically what happens when a nucleon in an atom's nucleus—the center—"decays" or breaks apart. If the nucleon was a neutron, then it becomes a proton, an electron, and an antineutrino. This is known as beta-minus (β-) decay. If the nucleon was a proton, then it breaks into a neutron, a positron, and a neutrino. This is beta-plus (β+) decay.

**electron**: One of the three components of an atom, electrons are the only parts not inside the nucleus. Instead, they orbit the nucleus like a cloud of moths around a porch light. Electrons have a negative electric charge.

**element**: A substance that can't be chemically separated into anything simpler. Some examples of common elements are hydrogen, carbon, oxygen, gold, and silver.

**hypothesis**: In science, the word *hypothesis* means an idea someone has thought of after doing a bunch of calculations and using logical inference.

This idea has not yet been tested. After the hypothesis has been thoroughly and carefully tested through a series of experiments, often by a number of different scientists, and all the results seem to confirm this idea, then the hypothesis becomes a scientific theory, something that has credibility.

**nucleon**: A nucleon can be a proton or a neutron, either of the individual components of an atom's nucleus.

**neutron**: Of the three parts that make up an atom, the neutron is the only one with no electric charge. Neutrons are found inside the nucleus of an atom, and, combined with protons, make up an element's atomic mass (weight).

**neutrino**: Not usually part of atoms, neutrinos can come out of atoms during beta decay. Neutrinos, like neutrons, have no electric charge and are almost massless. Their name is Italian for "little neutrons" because they are like tiny neutrons. They can also travel at or near the speed of light. Nothing else travels that fast besides photons (light particles).

**parity**: When physicists talk about parity, they talk about whether it is "conserved" or not. Parity is conserved when something and its mirror image react or respond in exactly the same way to outside influences; parity is about how symmetrical a system is.

**positron:** A positron is the antiparticle of an electron—sort of like the electron's opposite evil twin, except that it's not evil.

**proton**: The last of the three parts that make up an atom, protons can be found inside the nucleus with the neutrons. With a positive electric charge, a proton usually cancels out the negative electric charge of an electron in the same atom. The number of protons in an element is what gives the element its number on the periodic table.

## Further Reading

Camp, Carole Ann. *American Women of Science.* New Jersey: Enslow Publishers, Inc. 2001. pp. 58–67.

Cooperman, Stephanie H. *Chien-Shiung Wu: Pioneering Physicist and Atomic Researcher.* New York: The Rosen Publishing Group, Inc. 2004.

Di Domenico, Kelly. *Women Scientists Who Changed the World.* New York: The Rosen Publishing Group, Inc, Inc. 2012. pp. 47–54.

Sinnott, Susan. *Extraordinary Asian Americans and Pacific Islanders.* New York: Children's Press. 2003. pp. 101–103.

## Selected Bibliography

Chiang, Tsai-Chien. *Madame Wu Chien-Shiung: The First Lady of Physics Research.* Translated by Wong Tang-Fong. Singapore: World Scientific Publishing Co. Pte. Ltd. 2014.

Grinstein, Louise S., Rose K. Rose, and Miriam H. Rafailovich, eds. *Women in Chemistry and Physics.* Connecticut: Greenwood Press. 1993. pp. 613–625.

Lubkin, Gloria. "Chien-Shiung Wu, the First Lady of Physics Research." *Smithsonian,* Jan. 1971, pp. 52–57.

McGrayne, Sharon Bertsch. *Nobel Women in Science: Their Lives, Struggles, and Momentous Discoveries.* New Jersey: Carol Publication Group. A Birch Lane Press Book. 1993. pp. 255–279.

Stille, Darlene R. *Extraordinary Women Scientists.* Chicago: Children's Press. 1995. pp. 188–191.